In the Spotlight

Stephen Curry

by Kaitlyn Duling

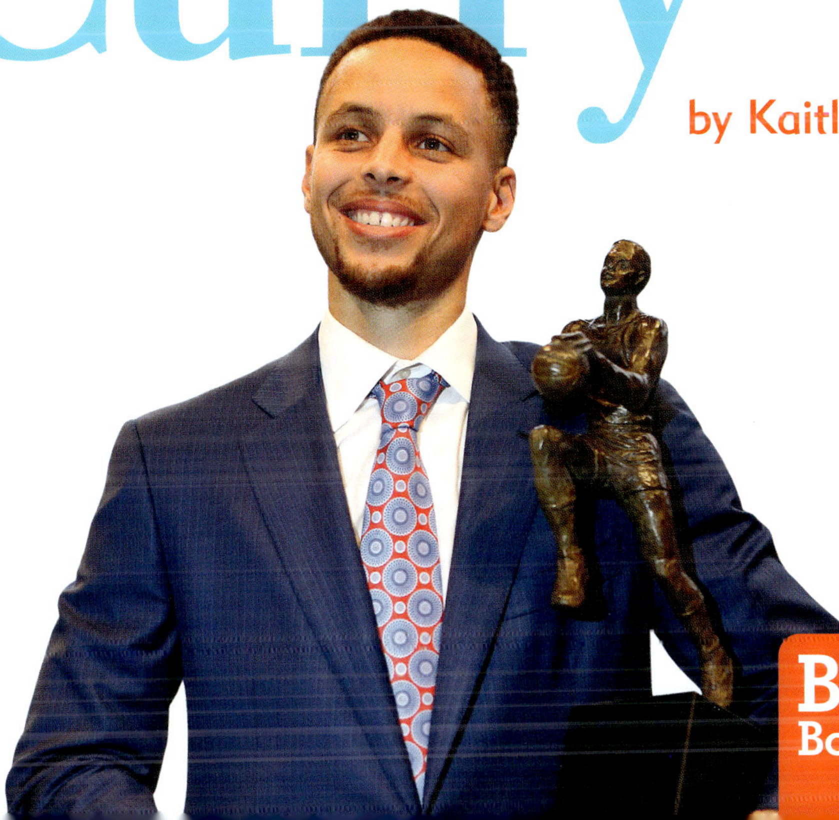

Bullfrog Books

Ideas for Parents and Teachers

Bullfrog Books let children practice reading informational text at the earliest reading levels. Repetition, familiar words, and photo labels support early readers.

Before Reading

- Discuss the cover photo. What does it tell them?
- Look at the picture glossary together. Read and discuss the words.

Read the Book

- "Walk" through the book and look at the photos. Let the child ask questions. Point out the photo labels.
- Read the book to the child, or have him or her read independently.

After Reading

- Prompt the child to think more. Ask: What did you know about Stephen Curry before reading this book? What more would you like to learn about him after reading it?

Bullfrog Books are published by Jump!
5357 Penn Avenue South
Minneapolis, MN 55419
www.jumplibrary.com

Library of Congress Cataloging-in-Publication Data

Names: Duling, Kaitlyn, author.
Title: Stephen Curry / by Kaitlyn Duling.
Description: Bullfrog Books edition.
Minneapolis, Minnesota : Jump!, Inc., [2019]
Series: In the Spotlight | Includes index.
Audience: Ages: 5–8. | Audience: Grades: K to Grade 3.
Identifiers: LCCN 2018014967 (print)
LCCN 2018017329 (ebook)
ISBN 9781641281942 (ebook)
ISBN 9781641281928 (hardcover : alk. paper)
ISBN 9781641281935 (paperback)
Subjects: LCSH: Curry, Stephen, 1988
Juvenile literature. | African American basketball players—United States—Biography—Juvenile literature. | Basketball players—United States
Biography—Juvenile literature.
Golden State Warriors (Basketball team)
History—Juvenile literature.
Classification: LCC GV884.C88 (ebook)
LCC GV884.C88 D85 2018 (print) | DDC 796.323092 [B]—dc23
LC record available at https://lccn.loc.gov/2018014967

Editors: Susanne Bushman & Kristine Spanier
Designer: Molly Ballanger

Photo Credits: Daniel Gluskoter/AP Images, cover, 1; Marcio Jose Sanchez/AP Images, 3, 6–7, 14–15, 18, 20–21, 23tl, 23br; McClatchy-Tribune/Alamy, 4, 19; Ezra Shaw/AP Images, 5, 23tr; Jeff Chiu/AP Images, 8–9, 23bl; Adm Golub/AP Images, 10; Bullit Marquez/AP Images, 11; Eric Kayne/AP Images, 12–13; ZUMA Press/Alamy, 16–17; Henryk Sadura/Shutterstock, 22tl; Ptapov Alexander/Shutterstock, 22tr; Ben Margot/AP Images, 22b; Jordan Strauss/AP Images, 24.

Printed in the United States of America at Corporate Graphics in North Mankato, Minnesota.

Table of Contents

Stephen

Who is this?
Stephen Curry!

We call him Steph.
He is famous. Why?

ELLIS
11
GOLDEN STATE
30
WARRIORS

He plays for the NBA!

He shoots baskets.

He scores points!

Steph is one of the best.

The NBA voted.

They said he was
the MVP!

When? 2015 and 2016.

MVP
award

He cares about kids.

He teaches them to play.

He helps people in need.

SCORE
EXIT
EOYDC
EAST OAKLAND YOUTH DEVELOPMENT CENTER
OF THE HOYAS

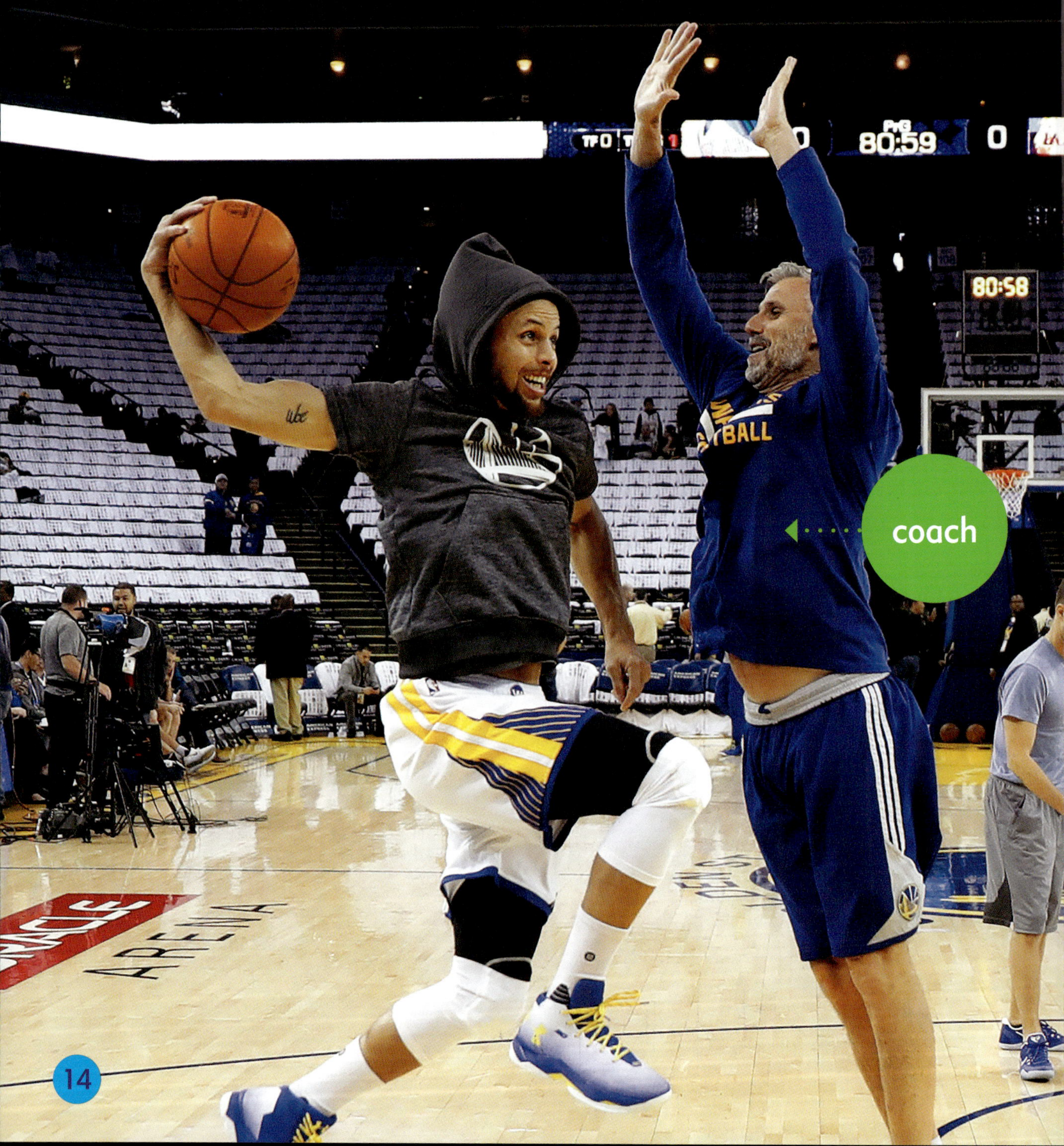
coach

Steph practices with his team.

He works with coaches, too.

He works hard!

He is a great player.
He loves to play!

GOLDEN STATE
30
WARRIORS
BLAZERS
1

What team does he play for? The Golden State Warriors. Cool!

They are champions!

They won the NBA Finals in 2017.

trophy
WARRIORS

They won in 2018, too.

Steph helps them win!

Will they win again?

Key Events

March 14, 1988:
Wardell Stephen Curry II is born in Akron, Ohio.

June 25, 2009:
The Golden State Warriors select Steph as the seventh pick in the NBA draft.

February 25, 2015:
Steph visits the White House. He gives a speech about preventing malaria, a disease spread by mosquitoes.

May 10, 2016:
Steph is announced the 2015–2016 MVP of the NBA.

July 2017:
Steph is the first NBA player to sign a contract worth more than $200 million.

June 8, 2018:
Steph and the Golden State Warriors beat the Cleveland Cavaliers to win their second straight NBA Finals championship.

Picture Glossary

coaches
People who train others in a sport or skill.

famous
Very well-known to many people.

MVP
Most Valuable Player; the award given to the best performing player each season.

NBA
National Basketball Association; the men's professional basketball league in North America.

Index

To Learn More

Finding more information is as easy as 1, 2, 3.

1. Go to www.factsurfer.com
2. Enter "StephenCurry" into the search box.
3. Click the "Surf" button to see a list of websites.